Baby Dragon and the Animal Olympics

Written by Eliza Jones

Illustrated by Mark Chambers

Collins

The Animal Olympics were coming up and
Baby Dragon was very excited.

Animal
Olympics

2

"Just remember that it doesn't matter who wins," said Mummy Dragon.

But Baby Dragon was worried about something else ...

All his friends had decided what event to do.

Wolf was doing the long run.

Penguin was diving.

Monkey was doing gymnastics.

But what could Baby Dragon do?

The animal Olympics came around and Baby
Dragon was sad as he had no event to do.

But suddenly, a tall pelican came up to him and said, "Baby Dragon, can you light the torch for us please?"

Baby Dragon was very happy.
He blew the fire from his mouth
and it was his job to do it every year.

11

Baby Dragon was very happy for his friends too, who won their races, and he won his own medal for "The Best Fire Breather".

13

The Animal Olympics

15

Ideas for reading

Written by Linda Pagett B.Ed (hons), M.Ed
Lecturer and Educational Consultant

Learning objectives: apply phonic knowledge and skills as the prime approach to reading and spelling unfamiliar words that are not completely decodable; identify the main events and characters in stories; make predictions showing an understanding of ideas, events and characters; retell stories, ordering events using story language

Curriculum links: PE: Games activities

High frequency words: were, very, who, but, his, what, do, could, as, had, came, him, he, too, their

Interest words: Olympics, diving, long run, gymnastics, medal

Resources: whiteboard, ICT

Word count: 143

Getting started

- Introduce the word *Olympics*, asking children what it means and what events are involved. Ask children if there are any events which they might like to be good at and make comparisons with school sports day.

- Read the blurb on the back cover, pointing to the words, then look at the cover image. What event do they think Baby Dragon will be competing in?

Reading and responding

- Demonstrate how to read pp2–5 and then encourage children to read independently, from the beginning.

- Discuss children's understanding of each sporting event as they turn the page, ensuring they know what each one involves.

- Hear children read individually, prompting and praising for using picture, context and phonic cues.

Returning to the book

- Discuss children's predictions of the event Baby Dragon would do in the Olympics. Were they correct?

- Using the model on pp14–15, demonstrate how to tell a story as though you had visited the Animal Olympics, e.g. *One day I went to the animal Olympics and I saw a penguin diving.* Encourage children to do this independently. Prompt more able children to add their own animals to the story.